ACHIEVE LEVEL 4

SCIENCE

Matthew Watson
Series Editor: **Richard Cooper**

PLEASE NOTE: THIS BOOK MAY NOT BE PHOTOCOPIED OR REPRODUCED AND WE APPRECIATE YOUR HELP IN PROTECTING OUR COPYRIGHT.

Rising Stars UK Ltd., 22 Grafton Street, London W1S 4EX

www.risingstars-uk.com

All facts are correct at time of going to press.

First published 2003
This edition 2008

Text, design and layout © Rising Stars UK Ltd.

First edition written by: Gerald Page
Educational consultants: John Stringer and Deborah Herridge
Project management: Cambridge Publishing Management Ltd.
Project editor: Diane Teillol
Illustrations: Tim Oliver and Clive Wakfer
Design: Neil Adcock
Cover design: Burville-Riley Partnership

All rights reserved. No part of this publication may be reproduced, stored in a retrieval system, or transmitted, in any form by any means, electronic, mechanical, photocopying, recording or otherwise, without the prior permission of Rising Stars Ltd.

British Library Cataloguing in Publication Data
A CIP record for this book is available from the British Library.

ISBN 978-1-84680-286-7

Printed by Craft Print International Ltd, Singapore

Contents

How to use this book	4
About the National Tests	6
Test techniques	8
Section 1: Level 3 – The tricky bits	10
Section 2: Life processes and living things	19
Section 3: Materials and their properties	28
Section 4: Physical processes	35
Section 5: Scientific Enquiry	48
Section 6: Breadth of study	54
Section 7: Key topics	57
Answers	61

How to use this book

What we have included:
- ★ Those topics at Level 3 that are trickiest to get right.
- ★ ALL Level 4 content so you know that you are covering all the topics that could come up in the test.
- ★ We have also put in a selection of our favourite test techniques, tips for revision and some advice on what the tests are all about, as well as the answers so you can see how well you are getting on.

GOOD LUCK!

1. **Introduction** – This section tells you what you need to do to achieve a Level 4. It picks out the key learning objective and explains it simply to you.

2. **Self-assessment** – Tick the face that best describes your understanding of this concept.

3. **Question** – The question helps you to learn by doing. It is presented in a similar way to a National Test question and gives you a real example to work with.

4. **Flow chart** – This shows you the steps to use when completing questions like this. Some of the advice appears on every flow chart (e.g. 'Read the question then read it again'). This is because this is the best way of getting good marks in the test.

5. **Key facts** – Important scientific facts and information to help you remember the things you need to think about when answering questions on the topic.

6. **Tip boxes** – These provide test hints and general tips on getting the best marks in the National Tests.

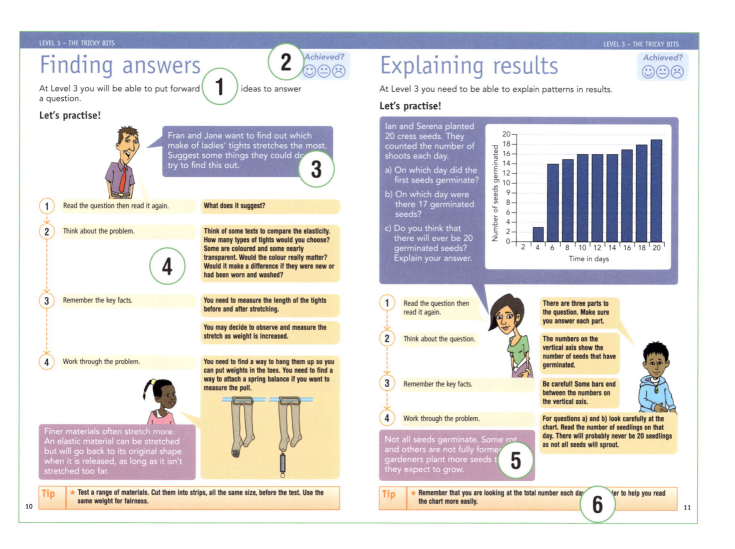

About the National Tests

Key facts

- The Key Stage 2 National Tests take place in the middle of May in Year 6. You will be tested on Maths, English and Science.
- The tests take place in your school and will be marked by examiners – not your teacher!
- You will get your results in July, two months after you take the tests.
- Most children will get a Level 4 or above, with about 30% getting to Level 5 (though this varies in each subject).
- Individual test scores are not made public but a school's combined scores are published in what are commonly known as league tables.

The Science National Tests

You will take two tests in Science, each one lasting 45 minutes. These are designed to test your knowledge and skills across the following areas of Science:

- Life processes and living things – the human body, plants and animals and their habitats.
- Materials and their properties – changing different materials, understanding the characteristics of different materials.
- Physical processes – electricity, forces, light and sound, the Sun and the Earth.
- Scientific Enquiry – ideas and evidence about Science and investigative skills.

DON'T FORGET!

Scientific Enquiry – The National Tests now include more questions that test your Scientific Enquiry skills.

The questions will often be based around a picture or a description of an investigation that children have carried out, along with their results. You won't need to carry out the investigation in the test but you might be asked how you would improve it if you were doing the investigation in class.

Recent National Tests papers included questions like:

- Work out the question that the children were investigating.
- Choose the best equipment to use in an investigation.
- Complete a table of results from an investigation.
- Draw conclusions from the results of investigations.
- Answer questions about graphs and charts completed in an investigation.
- Describe what the children have found out from an investigation.

You might also have to answer some questions about a famous scientist. In 2003 there was a series of questions about Edward Jenner. He found a cure for smallpox a long time ago and saved millions of lives!

Test techniques

Before the test

1. When you revise, try revising 'a little and often' rather than in long sessions.

2. Familiarise yourself with the key topics (pages 57–60) so you know what you need to do to get a Level 4. Information about other levels is given, so you can see the difference between them.

3. Revise with a friend. You can encourage and learn from each other.

4. Get a good night's sleep the night before.

5. Be prepared – bring your own pens and pencils.

During the test

1. READ THE QUESTION THEN READ IT AGAIN.

2. If you get stuck, don't linger on the same question – move on! You can come back to it later.

3. Never leave a multiple choice question. Make an educated guess if you really can't work out the answer.

4. Check to see how many marks a question is worth. Have you 'earned' those marks with your answer?

5. Check your answers after each question. Does your answer look correct?

6. Underline key words in the question.

⑦ Be aware of the time. After 20 minutes, check to see how far you have got.

⑧ Try to leave a couple of minutes at the end to check through what you have written.

⑨ Don't leave any questions unanswered. In the two minutes you have left yourself at the end, make an educational guess at the questions you really couldn't do.

⑩ You will have learned everything in the test. Think carefully – the information may be 'disguised' in another topic.

Things to remember

① Don't panic! If you see a difficult question, take your time, re-read it and have a go!

② Check every question and every page to be sure you don't miss any! Some questions will need two answers.

③ If a question is about measuring, always write in the UNIT of MEASUREMENT (e.g. newtons, l, kg).

④ Don't be afraid to ask a teacher for anything you need, such as tracing paper or another pencil.

⑤ Write neatly – if you want to change an answer, put a line through it and write beside the answer box.

⑥ Always double-check your answers.

⑦ Read through the whole paper when you've finished.

LEVEL 3 – THE TRICKY BITS

Finding answers

Achieved?

At Level 3 you will be able to put forward your own ideas to answer a question.

Let's practise!

> Fran and Jane want to find out which make of ladies' tights stretches the most. Suggest some things they could do to try to find this out.

1 Read the question then read it again. — **What does it suggest?**

2 Think about the problem. — **Think of some tests to compare the elasticity. How many types of tights would you choose? Some are coloured and some nearly transparent. Would the colour really matter? Would it make a difference if they were new or had been worn and washed?**

3 Remember the key facts. — **You need to measure the length of the tights before and after stretching. You may decide to observe and measure the stretch as weight is increased.**

4 Work through the problem. — **You need to find a way to hang them up so you can put weights in the toes. You need to find a way to attach a spring balance if you want to measure the pull.**

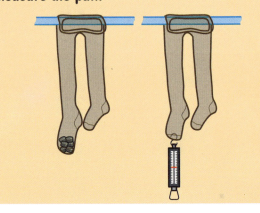

Finer materials often stretch more. An elastic material can be stretched but will go back to its original shape when it is released, as long as it isn't stretched too far.

| Tip | ★ Test a range of materials. Cut them into strips, all the same size, before the test. Use the same weight for fairness. |

LEVEL 3 – THE TRICKY BITS

Explaining results

Achieved?

At Level 3 you need to be able to explain patterns in results.

Let's practise!

Ian and Serena planted 20 cress seeds. They counted the number of shoots each day.

a) On which day did the first seeds germinate?

b) On which day were there 17 germinated seeds?

c) Do you think that there will ever be 20 germinated seeds? Explain your answer.

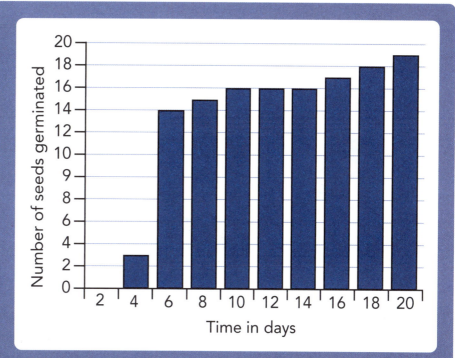

| 1 | Read the question then read it again. |

There are three parts to the question. Make sure you answer each part.

| 2 | Think about the question. |

The numbers on the vertical axis show the number of seeds that have germinated.

| 3 | Remember the key facts. |

Be careful! Some bars end between the numbers on the vertical axis.

| 4 | Work through the problem. |

For questions a) and b) look carefully at the chart. Read the number of seedlings on that day. There will probably never be 20 seedlings as not all seeds will sprout.

Not all seeds germinate. Some rot and others are not fully formed. Most gardeners plant more seeds than they expect to grow.

| Tip | ★ Remember that you are looking at the total number each day. Use a ruler to help you read the chart more easily. |

LEVEL 3 – THE TRICKY BITS

Living and non-living things

Achieved?

At Level 3 you will be able to describe the differences between living and non-living things.

Let's practise!

Join each sentence to the correct picture.

CHILD   It can move by itself.   DOLL

It does not eat.

It breathes.

It will grow into an adult.

It will not grow at all.

1 Read the question then read it again.

You are being asked to show the differences between living things and things that are not alive.

2 Remember the key facts.

Most living animals can:
- move
- eat
- grow (reproduce)
- respire
- use their senses
- get rid of waste

3 Work through the problem.

Join up the ones that you are sure about at first. Make sure you only draw one line from each sentence.

Everything on our planet can be divided into living and non-living things.

We need to be sure that an animal or plant is living by looking carefully to see whether it shows certain life processes.

All animals and plants can grow, move, reproduce and are sensitive to changes in their environment.

Plants make their own food, while animals have to move to find food to eat.

| Tip | ★ Compare a real pet cat with a toy cat. List what each one can and cannot do. Repeat with a caterpillar and a wooden toy caterpillar, and a car and a horse. |

LEVEL 3 – THE TRICKY BITS

Variables affecting plant growth

At Level 3 you will need to be able to say how changes affect plant growth. For example, this chart shows the effects of being in a different place.

Achieved?

Let's practise!

Harry grew three trays of cress seedlings. He gave them all the same amount of water. He put them in different places.

	Water each day	Place tray kept	Height of seedlings	Colour of seedlings
Tray A	3 spoons	On a windowsill	24 cm	Dark green
Tray B	3 spoons	In a cupboard	28 cm	Pale yellow and spindly
Tray C	3 spoons	In a shady part of the classroom	26 cm	Light green

a) Which seedlings grew the tallest?

b) Which seedlings were the shortest?

c) What was kept the same for each tray of seedlings?

d) What would be different about the cupboard compared to the windowsill?

1 Read the question then read it again.

The question has four parts. Look at the table and see what happened to each tray of seedlings.

2 Think about the question. What does the table tell you?

The third column in the table tells you how tall each plant was at the end of the experiment. The last column tells you how light affected the colouring of the plant and how healthy it looked. Everything is the same for each tray of seedlings, except for the place the seedlings grew.

3 Remember the key facts.

Plants don't grow as well if they are in the shade, or in complete darkness. Seedlings that grow in darkness will be spindly, yellow and pale, even though they are taller.

4 Work through the problem.

Remember what you know about plants' need for light.

Plants with some water grow better than plants which are dry. However, too much water kills plants.

13

LEVEL 3 – THE TRICKY BITS

Grouping materials

Achieved?

At Level 3 you will be able to group materials according to their properties.

Let's practise!

Here are the names of different materials:

wood   brass   plastic   steel

a) Write the correct material name in each box.

conducts electricity	does not conduct electricity

b) Draw a line from the material to the correct description.

steel
glass
iron
aluminium

magnetic

non-magnetic

① Read the question then read it again.

In the first part of the question you have to put each material into one group. Each material will go into one group or another. In the second part you must link each material with one description.

② Remember the key facts.

All metals conduct electricity. But not all metals are magnetic.

③ Work through the problem. What are the properties of these materials?

The property of the material may be different from the object made from it. For example, steel or glass will float if made into a boat shape.

The two most frequently used magnetic metals are iron and steel. No other common metals are magnetic.

Good electrical insulators include wood, plastic, air and glass.

Metals are good electrical conductors.

Tip ★ You may be asked to group materials based on their properties. For example, are they 'thermal conductors'? or 'thermal insulators'? Do they float? Do they sink?

LEVEL 3 – THE TRICKY BITS

Uses of materials

Achieved?

At Level 3 you will be able to say why different materials are used for special purposes.

Let's practise!

Join the name of the material to what it is like. Then join what it is like to what it can be used for. Glass has been done for you.

Material	What it is like	What it can be used for
Glass	Soft and warm to the touch	Bike tyres
Copper	Heavy and hard	Windows
Rubber	Transparent	Clothes
Cotton	Electrical conductor	Garden walls
Stone	High friction and hard wearing	Electrical wires

1 Read the question then read it again.

You have to complete two steps. Join the material to what it is like first. Make sure that each material is joined to a description. Now join one description to one use.

2 Remember the key facts. Think of everyday materials and the reasons that they are used for certain jobs.

Objects are made from materials. Don't confuse the material's properties with the objects that it can be made into. Glass, for instance, can be made into objects that are not transparent.

Aluminium – strong, light and conducts heat (pans).

Leather – bends and is strong (belts and shoes).

Paper – cheap and easy to make into sheets (writing paper).

Plastic – does not conduct heat (pan handles).

Polythene – light, flexible and easy to shape (carrier bags).

Silk – soft and smooth (shirts).

15

LEVEL 3 – THE TRICKY BITS

Reversible and non-reversible changes

Achieved?

At Level 3 you will be able to say which changes can be reversed and which cannot be reversed.

Let's practise!

Draw a line from the change to the correct group. Two have been done for you.

- burning wood
- freezing water ——— change which is reversible
- firing pottery in a kiln
- frying an egg
- baking a cake ——— change which is not reversible
- heating ice

1 Think about the question. What does it tell you?

You need to match each change with the right description. Think about whether you could easily get the original material back again.

2 Remember the key facts.

Some changes can be reversed easily. These are mainly changes that involve melting, freezing and dissolving.

Freezing is reversible because you can get the liquid back.

Dissolving a solid is reversible. The liquid can be evaporated, leaving the solid behind.

Burning a candle is not reversible because as the candle burns some wax particles react with oxygen in the air to produce water vapour, carbon dioxide gas, heat and light. The wax particles that seem to disappear are actually changing into other substances and so cannot be reformed.

Burning paper is not a reversible change because the ash cannot be made back into paper again. Also, material is lost to the air as a gas.

Baking is not reversible because it is impossible to get the bag of flour, butter or sugar out of the cooked cake.

Heating clay at a very high temperature in a kiln is not reversible because even if you break up the pottery you cannot get the clay back again.

LEVEL 3 – THE TRICKY BITS

How we see things

At Level 3 you will be able to explain that we see things when light from them enters our eyes.

Let's practise!

Here are three drawings that might help explain how we see things.

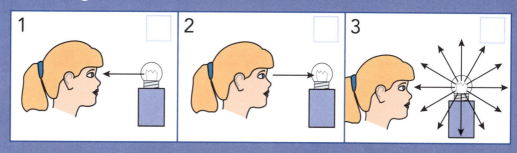

a) Tick the box next to the diagram you think shows the best way of describing how we see a candle.

b) Explain why you have chosen that diagram.

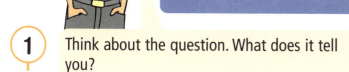

1 Think about the question. What does it tell you?

Each diagram is a way of thinking about how we see a bulb. You have to decide which seems best.

2 Remember the key facts.

Light travels from sources of light. Light travels away from the source in all directions. Only a small amount of the light produced enters our eyes.

3 Work through the problem.

- **The first idea is correct BUT it only shows one beam of light from the bulb. Is that all the light that is reflected?**
- **The second idea suggests that beams from the eye go to the bulb. This is not correct.**
- **The last idea is best because it shows light reflected in all directions. Only some of the light enters the eye of the person looking at the bulb.**

Light travels from sources such as the Sun, matches, candles, TV and stars. Some of the light they produce enters our eyes. Some of the light is reflected off other objects and this reflected light also enters our eyes, so we can see the object.

A periscope reflects light using two mirrors and lets us see over tall objects, such as hedges and fences. Drivers use mirrors to see what is behind them.

LEVEL 3 – THE TRICKY BITS

Pushes and pulls

Achieved?

At Level 3 you will be able to describe the effects of big and small pulls and pushes.

Let's practise!

a) Pulls are needed to move objects. Put these pulls in order from largest to smallest. Write in 1 next to the biggest pull and 4 next to the smallest.

b) Pushes are needed to move objects. Draw arrows to show the direction of the push in each picture.

1   Read the question then read it again.

There are four pushes and four pulls. Start with the biggest and then the smallest – these are easiest.

2   Remember the key facts.

Small objects often give small pushes and pulls. Large objects often give big pushes and pulls.

You should draw a force using a straight line with an arrowhead showing the direction of the force. The size or length of the arrow will depend on the size of the force.

Forces are measured using newtons (N).

Tip ★ There can be pushes and pulls even when objects are not touching. Magnets can pull (attract) or push (repel) over a distance. Gravity is a special pull force.

LIFE PROCESSES AND LIVING THINGS

Flower parts

Achieved?

At Level 4 you will be able to name the different parts of a flower.

Let's practise!

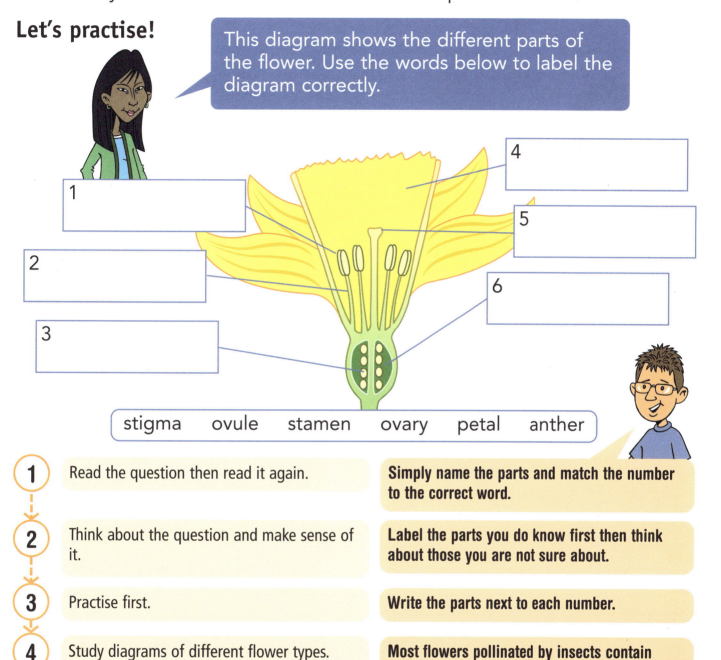

This diagram shows the different parts of the flower. Use the words below to label the diagram correctly.

1
2
3
4
5
6

stigma   ovule   stamen   ovary   petal   anther

1	Read the question then read it again.	**Simply name the parts and match the number to the correct word.**
2	Think about the question and make sense of it.	**Label the parts you do know first then think about those you are not sure about.**
3	Practise first.	**Write the parts next to each number.**
4	Study diagrams of different flower types.	**Most flowers pollinated by insects contain these parts.**

Anther – the tip of the flower's stamen, which contains pollen.

Ovary – the undeveloped seed. When the ovule is fertilised by the male pollen, the ovule becomes a seed.

Petal – the colourful outer part of the flower.

Stamen – the male part of the flower: the anther and its stalk.

Stigma – the tip of the female part of the flower. It receives the pollen grains.

Tip ★ staMEN – (male)   stigMA – (female – as in 'mum'!)

LIFE PROCESSES AND LIVING THINGS

Teeth and eating

Achieved?

At Level 4 you will be able to make comparisons of different types of teeth and identify their correct functions.

Let's practise!

Label the four main types of teeth.
Join each tooth name to its correct function.

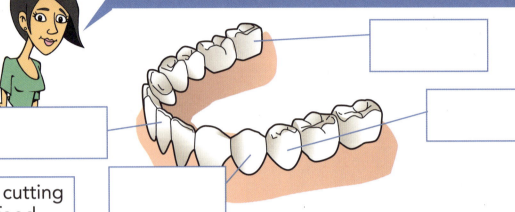

For cutting food

For grinding and crushing food

For holding and tearing food

For grinding and crushing food

1. Read the question then read it again.

There are two parts to the question. In the first part you simply have to label the diagram. In the second part you need to choose the correct use for the tooth.

2. Think about the question and make sense of it.

Start with the teeth names that you know for certain.

3. Work through the problem.

Two teeth types have the same function. Think about the key information that you have learned about the four main teeth types.

Teeth – break food into smaller pieces, then grind the food up before we swallow it.

Incisor teeth – for cutting food.

Canine teeth – for holding and tearing food.

Premolar and molar teeth – for grinding and crushing food.

Healthy teeth – it is important to brush your teeth at least twice a day and visit your dentist at least twice a year. Bacteria in your mouth convert sugar to acids, which can damage your teeth.

LIFE PROCESSES AND LIVING THINGS

Human organs

Achieved?

At Level 4 you will be able to name the major organs of the human body.

- skin
- lungs
- brain
- bladder
- stomach
- heart
- intestines
- liver
- kidneys

Draw a line from each word to the correct organ.

Let's practise!

1. Read the question then read it again.
2. Think about the question and make sense of it.
3. Work through the problem.

Look at the diagram before drawing any lines.

Your heart and lungs are in your chest. The other organs are in your abdomen or 'tummy'.

Your skin *surrounds* and protects all of your organs. It helps to control your temperature.

Bladder – stores urine (wee) before you go to the toilet.

Brain – receives information through the senses and then sends messages to your body to control its actions.

Heart – pumps blood so that every part of your body can receive food and oxygen.

Kidneys – make urine (wee) from waste products and excess water found in your blood.

Large intestines – changes food waste into faeces (poo).

Liver – an energy store and the body's main producer of chemicals.

Lungs – deliver oxygen to and remove carbon dioxide from your blood.

Skin – protects your body from damage, infection and drying out.

Small intestines – break up your food so that it can be taken up by your blood.

Stomach – stores food and mixes it with chemicals to break it down.

LIFE PROCESSES AND LIVING THINGS

Living processes

Achieved?

At Level 4 you will be able to show your understanding of living things.

Let's practise!

a) Which of these is the odd one out?

fish   tree   bonfire   badger

b) How do you know that plants are alive? List as many reasons as you can.

1 Read the question then read it again. — There are two parts to the question. Make sure you answer both.

2 Work through part a). — Remember the characteristics of most living things.

3 Work through part b). — Plants produce seeds, grow, use sunlight, water and oxygen to make food.

The life processes that plants go through take place more slowly than in animals and we might not always notice them.

Plant leaves turn slowly to catch as much sunlight as they can. Plants do not breathe in the way that animals like us do but they respire, they take in air and give out waste gases through their leaves.

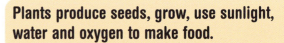

Most living things:
- move (even if very slowly)
- take in one gas and give out a different one
- sense and respond to the environment
- feed (plants make food using sunlight)
- grow
- reproduce (have babies or produce seeds)
- produce waste materials

LIFE PROCESSES AND LIVING THINGS

Classification

Achieved?

At Level 4 you will be able to put living things into groups.

Let's practise!

Look at these animals. Write their names in the correct groups below.

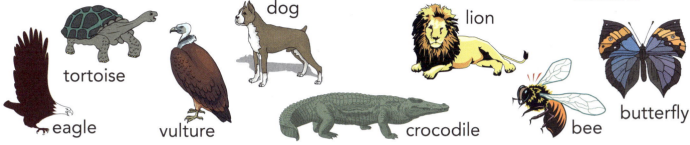

mammal	bird
reptile	insect

1. Read the question then read it again. — **Look carefully at each picture then match it to a group.**

2. Practise first. — **Remember the characteristics of each animal group.**

3. Study the question and make sense of it. — **There are eight animals and four animal groups. There will be more than one animal in some – or all – groups.**

Amphibians have smooth, moist skin. They live on land, but breed in water (frogs, newts, salamanders).

Birds have two legs, feathers and wings and lay eggs (blackbirds, eagles, ostriches).

Fish have gills and are covered in scales. They are cold blooded and live in water (goldfish, carps, sharks).

Insects have six legs and a body in three parts (butterflies, bees, beetles).

Mammals are warm blooded and have hair. Mammals give birth to their young alive and feed them on milk (mice, elephants, humans).

Reptiles are cold blooded, have an outer covering of scales or plates and they lay eggs (lizards, tortoises, turtles).

LIFE PROCESSES AND LIVING THINGS

Keys

At Level 4 you will be able to use and construct keys to put living things into groups.

Let's practise!

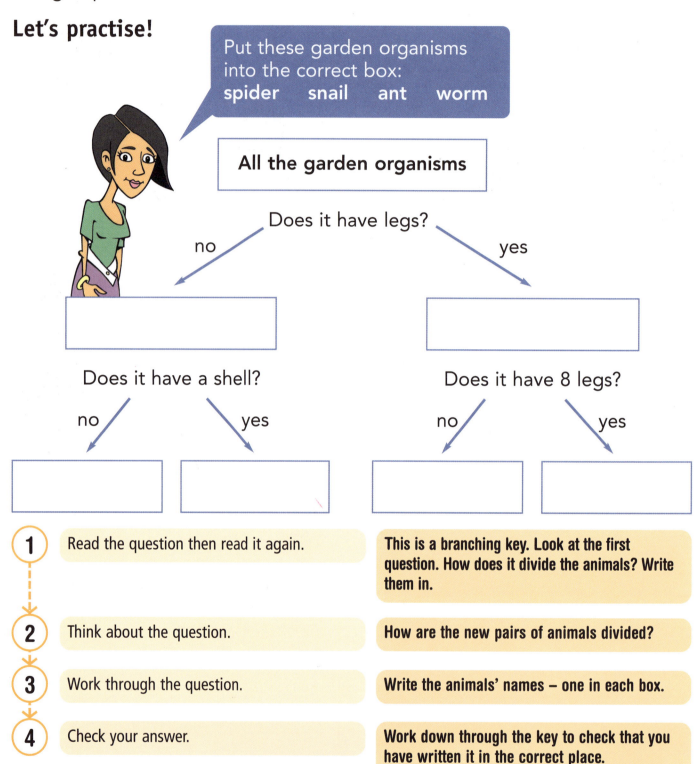

Put these garden organisms into the correct box:
spider   snail   ant   worm

All the garden organisms

Does it have legs?
no — yes

Does it have a shell?
no / yes

Does it have 8 legs?
no / yes

1. Read the question then read it again.

   This is a branching key. Look at the first question. How does it divide the animals? Write them in.

2. Think about the question.

   How are the new pairs of animals divided?

3. Work through the question.

   Write the animals' names – one in each box.

4. Check your answer.

   Work down through the key to check that you have written it in the correct place.

A key is made up of a number of questions; each one will divide a large group into two smaller groups. This continues until you are left with each organism on its own so that you can identify it.

LIFE PROCESSES AND LIVING THINGS

Animals in their environment

Achieved?

At Level 4 you will be able to say how some animals are adapted to their habitat.

Let's practise!

Information from an encyclopedia has become mixed up. Can you join the animal to where it lives and how it has adapted to its habitat?

Animal	Where it lives	Adaptation
shark	grasslands	… long neck so that they can feed from tree tops … … have tough tongues which allow them to pull leaves from trees without being hurt by thorns … … have a camouflaged pattern to allow them to blend in …
penguin	oceans	… long eyelashes to keep sand out … … feet are wide so that they don't sink … … body colours allow them to blend in … … can store fat in their hump …
camel	icy land and cold seas	… streamlined body … … able to detect vibrations made by animals … … can smell prey from long distances …
giraffe	desert	… waterproof feathers … … insulating blubber … … paddle-like feet …

1 Read the question then read it again.

There are two main parts to this question. In each part there are four lines to draw.

2 Practise first.

Draw the lines faintly to start with until you are sure that your answers are correct.

3 Study the question and make sense of it.

Think about where each animal lives. How is it adapted to that environment?

The place where an animal lives is called a **habitat**.
Animals and plants must be well adapted to the conditions of their environment to survive.

25

LIFE PROCESSES AND LIVING THINGS

Predators and prey

Achieved?

At Level 4 you will be able to recognise food chains.

Let's practise!

Draw an arrow from the prey to the predator.

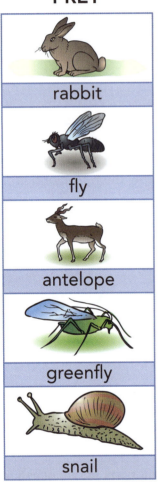

PREY

- rabbit
- fly
- antelope
- greenfly
- snail

PREDATOR

- fox
- spider
- lion
- ladybird
- thrush

1	Read the question then read it again.	In this question you should try to connect each predator to its prey.
2	Think about the question.	*Prey* are animals that are eaten. *Predators* are animals that eat other animals.
3	Remember the key facts.	Prey are the animals that are eaten by predators. Arrows are always drawn *towards* the predator.
4	Work through the problem.	Look at each predator in turn and work out which animal it is likely to eat.

LIFE PROCESSES AND LIVING THINGS

Food chains

Achieved?

At Level 4 you will be able to describe food chains.

Let's practise!

This is an example of a food chain.

All food chains start with the Sun.

Sun ➡ grass ➡ sheep ➡ human

a) Use the words below to make a food chain of your own. Remember to draw the arrows facing in the correct direction, from left to right.

rabbit   grass   fox   Sun

b) Complete the food chain below using a common animal.

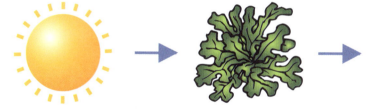

| Sun | lettuce | | thrush |

1. Read the question then read it again.

   Food chains show different feeding relationships. The arrow shows the way the food is moving.

2. Remember the key facts.

   All food chains start with the Sun. This is the main source of energy. After the Sun, most food chains contain a green plant.

3. Think of examples you know.

   Start with the Sun and next will be the grass as this is the producer in the chain. Once you have worked out that the fox will eat the rabbit, you will be able to complete the chain.

Green plants are called **producers** because they produce food for the rest of the chain. The rest of the organisms in the chain are called **consumers**.

27

MATERIALS AND THEIR PROPERTIES

Thermal insulators and conductors

Achieved?

At Level 4 you will know that heat passes through some materials more easily than through others.

Let's practise!

Jo has filled three cups with hot tea. One cup is polystyrene, one is pottery and one is metal.

- The metal cup feels hot.
- The pottery cup feels warm.
- The polystyrene cup is only slightly warm.

Explain why the cups feel different.

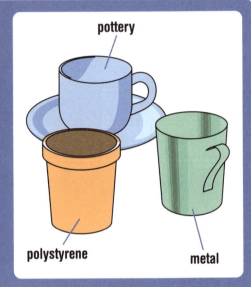

1. Read the question then read it again. — What is the important difference between the cups?

2. Think about the question. What does it tell you? — The heat must have come from the hot tea.

3. Think about real-life examples. — Remember your own experiences with hot drinks.

4. Remember the key facts. — Heat travels through some materials better than others.

5. Work through the problem. — Heat must travel easily through the metal. If heat can travel easily through a material, then that material is a good thermal conductor.

Material – what objects are made from.

Metals – good conductors of heat.

Wood and **polystyrene** – very poor conductors of heat (also called thermal insulators).

Good thermal conductors let heat through more easily than poor thermal conductors.

MATERIALS AND THEIR PROPERTIES

Gases

Achieved?

At Level 4 you will be able to recognise that gases have different properties that help us to separate them from solids and liquids. You will know that there are many types of gases, including carbon dioxide and helium.

Let's practise!

Tick the correct statements.
- [ ] Gases do not flow.
- [ ] Gases take the shape of their container.
- [ ] Gases keep the same volume.
- [ ] Gases fill the space available.
- [ ] Gases stay the same shape.

1. Read the question then read it again.

   This question is about states of matter. Materials can either be gas, liquid or solid. This question is about gases.

2. Think about the question. What does it tell you?

   How do gases differ from solids and liquids?

3. Remember the key facts about gases. Think about everyday examples, such as perfume.

   You cannot cut, or shape, or pour a gas.

Air is a mixture that includes nitrogen, oxygen, carbon dioxide and some water vapour.

Carbon dioxide dissolves in water to make drinks fizzy.

Helium is a very light gas so helium balloons float in air.

Natural gas burns easily.

Remember	★ Gases are everywhere. We breathe them all the time. • Divers breathe air in tanks when underwater • Astronauts take air with them into space. • Some harmful gases come out of car exhausts.

MATERIALS AND THEIR PROPERTIES

Making mixtures

Achieved?

At Level 4 you will be able to describe the changes that occur when materials are mixed.

Let's practise!

Tim added four materials to water.

a) Tick the boxes of the materials that dissolved.

- ☐ salt — after a minute the mixture was transparent
- ☐ gravel — all the gravel sank to the bottom
- ☐ flour — the mixture was cloudy
- ☐ brown sugar — the mixture was transparent and brown coloured

Tim then tried different ways to make them dissolve more quickly.

b) Tick the things that helped the materials dissolve more quickly.

- ☐ stir the mixture
- ☐ use hot water
- ☐ use more water
- ☐ use more solid

(1) Read the question then read it again.

In the first part all the information is in the question. In the second part (how to speed up dissolving) you have to rely on what you already know.

(2) Remember the key facts.

When a mixture *dissolves* in water you can no longer see it. It leaves the water *transparent*. Coloured solids will colour the water when they dissolve.

(3) Work through the problem.

Stirring and using *warm water* speed up dissolving.

MATERIALS AND THEIR PROPERTIES

Separating mixtures

Achieved?

At Level 4 you will know about the ways to separate simple mixtures.

Let's practise!

Ali made a solution of salt and water. After a few minutes stirring she could no longer see the salt. She left it in a saucer on the radiator overnight. Next day the water had gone and she was left with the salt in the saucer. What happened to the salt and water when she stirred it? What happened to the water overnight?

1 Read the question then read it again.

You cannot filter salt from water. You need another method.

2 Think about the question. What does it tell you?

This solution is a mixture of salt and water. To get the solid salt back Ali has to get rid of the water.

3 Remember the key facts.

Salt dissolves in water. If you let the water evaporate the salt will be left behind.

4 Work through the problem.

The water has evaporated. The dissolved solid – salt – has been left behind.

Ways to separate mixtures

Filter – a filter is a kind of mini-sieve. If you look at filter paper through a microscope you will see that it has many tiny holes which only allow liquids (such as water) and dissolved substances through.

Magnets – you could use a magnet to separate iron filings or steel paper clips from other solids, such as sand, soil or pasta.

Sieve – use this to separate most undissolved solids from a liquid, or to separate two solids of different size.

Dissolve – when a solid dissolves in water its tiny particles cannot be seen.

Evaporate – this happens when a liquid turns to a gas. Any dissolved solids are left behind.

Solution – a mixture formed when a solid dissolves.

MATERIALS AND THEIR PROPERTIES

Sieving and filtering

Achieved?

At Level 4 you will need to know about ways to separate mixtures by sieving and filtering.

Let's practise!

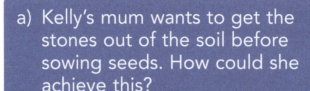

a) Kelly's mum wants to get the stones out of the soil before sowing seeds. How could she achieve this?

b) Bill wants to get the 'bits' out of his freshly squeezed orange juice. He tried a sieve but the bits went straight through the holes. He used filter paper instead. Explain how the filter paper worked.

1 Read the question then read it again.

There are two parts to this question. The first deals with removing solids from solids and the second deals with removing solids from liquids.

2 Think about the question. What does it tell you?

To remove the stones you would sieve the soil mixture. The soil will go through the holes in the sieve, while the stones won't.

3 Think of other examples.

The holes in the sieve were too big to trap the 'bits' in the orange juice so Bill used filter paper. The paper will let the juice through, but stop the bits, which will be left on the paper.

You can use a sieve to sort particles of different sizes. This is what Kelly's mum is doing.

You can use filter paper to separate very small particles (such as sand) which can't be easily removed by a sieve because the holes are too large.

Tips
★ Dissolved substances will pass through filter paper because the particles are smaller than the holes in the filter paper.
★ When solid particles are not dissolved the filter paper traps them but allows the water to pass through.

MATERIALS AND THEIR PROPERTIES

Solid, liquid and gas

Achieved?

At Level 4 you will be able to group materials into solids, liquids or gases.

Let's practise!

a) Write the name of each of these materials in the correct column.

stone   oxygen   paper   milk   shampoo
helium   chocolate   hydrogen   ice cream   oil

Solid at room temperature	Liquid at room temperature	Gas at room temperature

b) Think about your breakfast. Can you name two foods that are solid? Did you eat or drink any that are liquid?

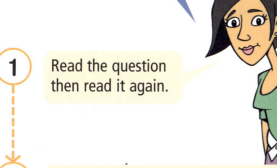

1. Read the question then read it again.

2. Remember the key facts.

Write the name of the material in the correct column. When it comes to the breakfast question, cereals, sugar and milk are a good starting point.

- Solids will not run and can be cut into pieces.
- Liquids are runny but stay in a container or on a surface.
- Gas escapes to fill any container.

Solids stay the same shape and keep the same volume.

Liquids flow, they take the shape of their container and keep the same volume.

Gases flow, they take the shape of their container and they fill the container because they have no definite volume.

Tip	★ Some liquids, like shampoo, run slowly.

33

MATERIALS AND THEIR PROPERTIES

Evaporation

At Level 4 you will know about the factors that affect the way liquids evaporate.

Let's practise!

Kamal wanted to find out if water would evaporate at different speeds in different places.

He put 100 ml of water into three different containers.

He left one container on a sunny windowsill for two days.

He put another in a warm cupboard. The third went in the fridge.

a) From which container did the water evaporate most quickly/least quickly?

b) Why was there a difference?

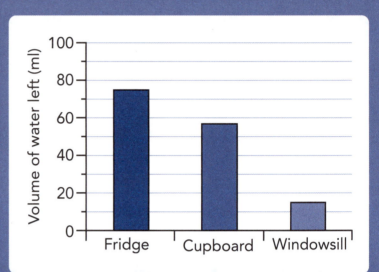

1. Read the question then read it again.

The question assumes you know that water evaporates. This happens when water from the surface changes to a *gas*. There seems to be a difference between the way water *evaporates* at different temperatures. You are asked to spot the differences from the bar chart and then explain the difference.

2. Think about the question. What does it tell you?

Water evaporates at a different rate from a container kept in one place compared to a container kept in a different place.

3. Remember the key facts.

Water will evaporate more quickly from a container in a warm place. All the containers are uncovered.

Evaporation is the loss of a material into the atmosphere.

Tips
★ If you do this experiment in the classroom, make sure the containers start with the same amount of water. Always use containers of the same size.
★ A 'factor' is something you can change.

PHYSICAL PROCESSES

Air resistance

Achieved?

At Level 4 you will be able to say that air resistance pushes against a moving object as it passes through air, slowing the object down.

Let's practise!

a) Bob drops two sheets of paper. One is flat and the other is scrunched into a ball. He drops them at the same time from the same height. Which one do you think will hit the ground first? Explain your idea.

b) Meena uses scrap writing paper to make balls. She makes one ball small and tight. She makes one large and loose. She throws the balls. Which ball do you think she will be able to throw furthest? Explain your idea.

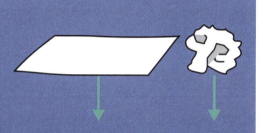

①	Read the question then read it again.	**These questions are connected because they are about air resistance and surface area.**
②	Think about the question. What does it tell you?	**In both cases one of the objects has a larger surface area, and so has more air resistance than the other.**
③	Remember the key facts.	**Air resistance *slows down* objects that fall or move through the air. The larger the size of the surface, the more the object is affected by air resistance.**
④	Work through the problem.	**The flat sheet will have far more air resistance than the screwed-up ball. This will mean that it is *affected* more by air resistance. It will fall more slowly. When Meena throws the balls, the large loose one will be slowed down more by air resistance.**

Another force that slows things down is 'water resistance'. When you walk through water you can feel water pushing against you. Air resistance isn't as strong as water resistance.

Tip	★ A big parachute will slow down an object more than a small one.

PHYSICAL PROCESSES

Magnetic attraction and repulsion

Achieved?

At Level 4 you have to know about magnetic forces. For example, two magnets will push each other away (repel each other) if the ends are the same poles. The two magnets will pull towards each other (attract) if the ends have different poles.

Let's practise!

Paula had two bar magnets. Each magnet had a blue end and a red end.

Red = North and Blue = South.

- What happens if she moves the red and blue ends together?
- If she moves the two blue ends together?
- If she moves the two red ends together?

① Read the question then read it again.

The red end attracts the blue.

② Think about the question. What does it tell you?

**There is a force pushing *like* ends apart.
There is a force pulling *unlike* ends together.**

③ Remember the key facts.

Like poles (the same) repel and unlike (different) poles attract.

④ Work through the problem.

The like poles will repel each other. The unlike poles will attract.

| Tip | ★ Always use the correct words about magnets:
Poles are the ends of the magnet.
Attract is the correct word. Do not say 'stick'.
Repel is the correct word for 'push apart'.
like = the same   unlike = different |

The red and blue ends are the *poles* of the magnet. The magnetic force of a magnet is concentrated in the poles.

PHYSICAL PROCESSES

Magnetic sorting

Achieved?

At Level 4 you have to know which metals are magnetic and which are not.

Let's practise!

Ravi tests materials to see which are attracted to a magnet. He sorts them into two sets. He lists the different metals.

Metal – used for	Does it conduct electricity?	Is it attracted to magnets?
aluminium – foil	✓	✗
steel – scissors	✓	✓
copper – pipes	✓	✗
silver – rings	✓	✗
iron – nails	✓	✓

List the metals that are magnetic and list the metals that are not magnetic.

1. Read the question then read it again.

   Some metals are attracted to magnets. Iron and steel are common magnetic metals.

2. Think about the question. What does it tell you?

   Are all metals magnetic? Do all metals conduct electricity? Record your knowledge.

3. Remember the key facts.

   Iron and steel are the only magnetic metals in the list.

4. Work through the problem.

Metals attracted to magnets	Metals not attracted to magnets
iron	copper
steel	silver
	aluminium

Other magnetic materials are nickel and cobalt.

Tip ★ When testing metals, if one is attracted to a magnet it must have iron or steel in it. 'Tin' cans only have a very thin coat of tin over a steel body.

37

PHYSICAL PROCESSES

Making electrical circuits

At Level 4 you will be able to describe and explain the way electrical devices, such as bulbs and cells, are connected in a circuit. You will also be able to explain about the changes that you could make to the devices to affect the brightness of the bulbs.

Let's practise!

Describe the bulbs in each of the circuits below using the following words. The first one has been done for you. Explain why the bulbs in these circuits appear different.

normal   bright   dim   off

1 Normal

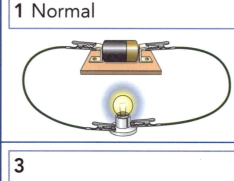

2

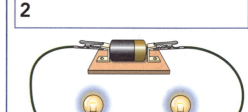

3

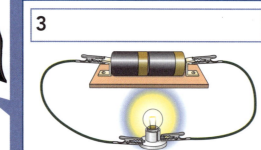

4

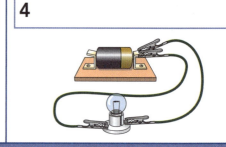

(1) Read the question then read it again.

Look carefully at the circuit that provides the 'normal' brightness of bulb. Remember the number of devices in the circuit.

(2) Think about the question. What does it tell you?

In Circuit 2 there are twice as many bulbs, but there is still only one cell. Think about the effect that this will have on the brightness of the bulbs. In Circuit 3, there are two cells and only one bulb and in Circuit 4 you need to look carefully at the way that the cell is connected.

(3) Work through the problem.

Which bulb is bright, which is dim and which is off?

| Tip | ★ If there is not a complete pathway, then the electricity will not flow and the bulb will not glow. |

PHYSICAL PROCESSES

Electrical switches

Achieved?

At Level 4 you will describe and explain the way electrical devices, such as switches, are connected in a circuit.

Let's practise!

Karen connected a switch into three circuits.

a) Tick the box next to the circuits where the bulb is glowing. Put a cross in the box next to the circuits where the bulb is not glowing.

1) 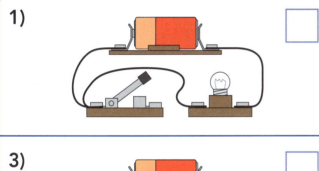 ☐

2) 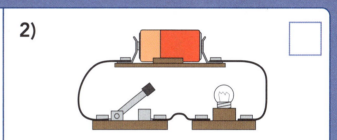 ☐

3) 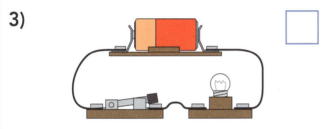 ☐

4) 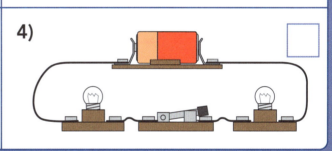 ☐

b) Explain why you have ticked or crossed each circuit.

1	Read the question then read it again.	There are two parts to this question. Make sure you answer both parts.
2	Think about the question.	The most important part of the drawings is the switch. Look carefully at the way it is connected.
3	Remember the key facts.	For electricity to flow, the circuit must be complete.
4	Work through the problem.	If the switch is open then electricity cannot pass through. Follow the path for the electricity all round the circuit. If the circuit is not complete then the electrical current will not flow and the bulb will not glow.

A switch is a way of making and breaking a circuit. An open switch uses air or an insulator to stop the electricity flowing.

Tip ★ In circuit 1), the switch is not part of the circuit so the bulb lights.

39

PHYSICAL PROCESSES

The position of the Sun

At Level 4 you will be able to describe the way the Sun appears to move.

Let's practise!

These three drawings show the shadow of a pole at different times on a sunny day.

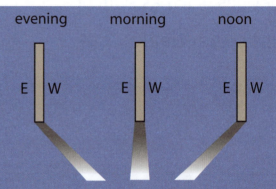

a) Match the correct time of the day to each shadow.

b) Why do the shadows change during the day? Tick one box.

☐ The Sun moves round the Earth.

☐ The Sun moves across the sky during the day.

☐ The Earth turns on its axis.

1 Read the question then read it again.

There are two parts. Draw the line first. Now think about explaining why shadows change.

2 Think about the question. What does it tell you?

Shadows change during the day. The reason for this may not be obvious.

3 Remember the key facts.

In the mornings and evenings the Sun appears to be low in the sky and the shadows are long. At midday (noon) the Sun appears to be high in the sky and the shadows are short.

4 Work through the problem.

Decide which of the drawings is noon (short shadow). In the morning the shadow will be cast from east to west because the Sun rises in the east and the evening shadow will be cast from west to east because the sun sets in the west.

The Earth rotates on its axis. This causes day and night. We say the Sun rises in the east and sets in the west and it appears to move across the sky each day, although it is really the Earth that is moving.

Tip ★ Remember to think about looking SOUTH when talking about the Sun's movement. East is then to your left and west is to your right. You can tell which direction south is because the Sun will be shining from that direction at lunchtime. You can record the shadows cast using a stick and chalk. The shadow will be on the opposite side of the stick to the Sun.

PHYSICAL PROCESSES

Gravity

Achieved?

At Level 4 you will be able to describe the effects of the pull of gravity.

Let's practise!

Ann is weighing objects with a spring balance. She records the weight of each object in a chart.

a) Which object weighs the most?
b) What units do we use for weight?
c) What is the force that pulls down on the objects?

Object	Weight (newtons)
drinks bottle	6
scissors	0.5
boots	4
tub of clay	13

1 Read the question then read it again. — Most of the information you need is in the table.

2 Picture the question. What does it tell you? — Think about which of these objects is heaviest. Which object stretched the string most?

3 Remember the key facts. — The pull of the Earth's gravity on objects is measured as their weight. When you step on a balance that shows your weight, you are squashing a spring. If you are heavy you will squash the spring a lot. If you are light the spring will be squashed less.

4 Work through the problem. — Look carefully at the table. The units of weight are shown at the top of the second column (newtons or N).

Gravity pulls objects. The force of gravity on an object can either squash or stretch a spring.

Tip ★ All objects have a force of gravity. In most cases, the bigger the object, the greater the force of gravity. The largest object that is close to us is the planet Earth. The pull of gravity depends on where you are. If you are on the Moon there is less gravity and you weigh less.

PHYSICAL PROCESSES

Friction

Achieved?

To achieve Level 4 you will know that forces stop objects moving. For example, friction will stop a book from sliding down a shallow slope.

Let's practise!

Look at this drawing. The toy car is not moving. Jim thinks that the toy just won't move. Rashid thinks the toy won't move because of air resistance acting against it. Sara thinks it will not move because of friction.

a) Who do you think is correct?

b) Why do you think so?

1. Read the question then read it again.

2. Think about the question. What does it tell you?

3. Think of an everyday example, such as a bike or skis on different surfaces.

Friction is the force stopping the toy car from moving

Gravity is pulling the car down the slope

Put a toy on a tray. It will only move when one end of the tray is lifted.

Air resistance – the force that pushes against a moving object as it passes through air, slowing the object down.

Friction – a force which stops things moving against or through each other.

Surface friction – when a solid slides against another solid.

| Tip | ★ *Gravity* pulls on all objects.
Air resistance slows the fall of an object that falls through the air. |

PHYSICAL PROCESSES

Friction forces

Achieved? 😀 😐 😞

At Level 4 you will be able to explain how moving things are affected by forces like friction.

Let's practise!

Kate made a slide out of cotton for her toy. She attached the toy to the slide with a paperclip. She let it slide down the cotton runway.

a) What force pulled the toy down the slide?

b) She made a second slide out of rough string. What do you think will happen to the toy? Explain your idea.

1. Read the question then read it again. — There are two parts to the question. Make sure you answer each part.

2. Think about the question. What does it tell you? — The slide was made of cotton and it was sloping downwards.

3. Remember the key facts.  Gravity pulls objects towards the Earth. The fact that they go down a slope does not change this. Whenever an object moves, it is slowed by friction. This is caused by rubbing between two surfaces. The cotton is smooth so the force of friction is reduced.

4. Work through the problem. — Gravity pulled the toy down the slide. The rough string will have more friction. The toy may slide more slowly – or it may not slide at all!

Tip ★ There is always friction when two surfaces move against each other. A simple way to create friction is to rub your hands together. Some smooth surfaces are still high friction. Think of bike brakes!

PHYSICAL PROCESSES

The size of shadows

At Level 4 you will be able to describe the way shadows change.

Let's practise!

The clown is in the spotlight.

The spotlight is moved higher up. The clown stays where he is. What happens to the clown's shadow?

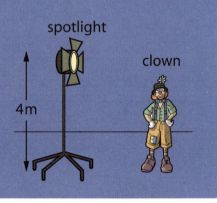

1 Read the question then read it again.

The lamp is higher. What difference will that make to the shadow?

2 Think about the question. What does it tell you?

When the position of the light changes so does the shadow.

3 Remember the key facts.

Light travels in straight lines. A line from the spotlight to the top of the clown will show you where the shadow will be on the floor.

4 Work through the problem.

Notice the difference in the length of the shadow. When the light source is moved, the shadow changes.

Shadows are formed when light is blocked.

When a light source is directly overhead we see no shadow. Shadows are longest when the light is at a shallow angle.

| Tip | ★ Practise making shadows with a small toy and a torch. How many ways can you find to make the shadow bigger and smaller? |

PHYSICAL PROCESSES

Opaque, transparent and translucent

Achieved?

At Level 4 you will know that light will pass through transparent and translucent materials and not through those which are opaque.

Let's practise!

Leo and Ravi hold a book and an empty clear bottle in front of light.

The book makes a dark shadow.

The bottle makes a faint shadow.

a) Explain why one of the shadows is dark and the other is faint.

b) In the boxes below write **T** if the object is transparent, **TL** if the object is translucent and **O** if the object is opaque.

- [ ] glass window
- [ ] brick wall
- [ ] bathroom window
- [ ] mirror
- [ ] jam jar
- [ ] tissue paper

1	Read the question then read it again.	It is asking about the way light passes through some objects but not others.
2	Think about the question. What does it tell you?	Light is being *blocked* by one of the objects in the first part of the question. Light is passing through the other object.
3	Remember the key facts.	*Transparent* means that light will pass through it. *Opaque* means that light will be blocked. *Translucent* means that some light will pass through, but that you won't be able to see detailed shapes or lines.
4	Work through the problem.	Which materials are transparent and which are opaque? Transparent materials do not make much of a *shadow*.

Tip ★ Don't think that all solid things are opaque. The two words have very different meanings. Glass is one example of a transparent solid. Translucent means a surface that allows light to pass through it without showing the detailed shapes or lines of objects on the other side (for example, frosted glass in bathrooms).

45

PHYSICAL PROCESSES

Sounds we hear

Achieved?

At Level 4 you will be able to say how sounds are made when an object vibrates and how sound travels to our ears.

Let's practise!

Jim taps a triangle. It vibrates and makes a sound. How can Jim stop it vibrating?

Jim puts a few beads on the skin of the drum. He uses the drum sticks to tap it. Explain what happens.

Emma is working on the opposite side the classroom. She still hears Jim's drumming but it is faint. Explain why she hears the drum more faintly than Jim.

1 Read the question then read it again.

This question is about vibrations and about how vibrations travel through the air to our ears.

2 Think about the question. What does it tell you?

It is about how two different musical instruments vibrate and how sound is affected by distance.

3 Remember the key facts.

Sound is caused by the object vibrating. Sound gets fainter the further you are away from the source. Sound travels in all directions but gets fainter with distance.

4 Work through the problem.

Sound travels in waves. The triangle vibrates, which causes the air to vibrate and it is these vibrations that enter your ear.

Percussion instruments are those which vibrate after being tapped. In other musical instruments, strings, reeds, or even a column of air vibrate.

PHYSICAL PROCESSES

Sounds through different materials

Achieved?

At Level 4 you will be able to say how sound travels through different materials.

Let's practise!

a) Leo asks Kate to scratch the table gently. He can hardly hear her. What is the sound travelling through to reach his ear?

b) He puts his ear to the table. He can hear much better now. Explain this.

c) He puts a scarf between his ear and the table. He cannot hear the scratching at all now.
Explain why the sound is not reaching his ear.

1	Read the question then read it again.	It is about sound travelling differently through different materials.
2	Think about the question. What does it tell you?	How is Leo listening differently? What is the material conducting the sound each time.
3	Remember the key facts.	Sound has to travel through something. It can travel through: *gases* – we know this because air is a mixture of gases *liquids* – whales and dolphins communicate underwater using sound *solids* – when we use string telephones, the sound travels down the solid string
4	Work through the problem.	The scarf is a solid but it is very soft and fluffy. Sounds travel well through hard solids like the table – soft materials absorb sound and do not transmit it well.

Tip ★ Think about the old cowboy films. Trackers would put their ear to the ground to try to detect the sound of horses' hooves as sound travels better through rock than through the air.

SCIENTIFIC ENQUIRY

Questions in an experiment

Achieved? 😊 😐 ☹

At Level 4 you will have to decide which questions to investigate.

Let's practise!

Pat is testing different-sized parachutes.
She made all the parachutes from the same type of plastic.

a) Which question was she investigating?
   Tick the correct box.

   ☐ Do heavy parachutes fall more slowly?
   ☐ Do parachutes with a larger surface area fall more slowly than those with a smaller surface area?
   ☐ Do plastic parachutes fall more slowly than paper ones?
   ☐ Do red parachutes fall more slowly than yellow ones?

b) This table shows the results of her test.

Area of the parachute	100 cm²	200 cm²	250 cm²
Time taken to fall 1 m	2 seconds	4 seconds	5 seconds

c) Explain the pattern you can see.

1	Read the question then read it again.	There are two parts. In the first part you have to decide what she wanted to find out. In the second part you have to use her table of results.
2	Think about the question. What does it tell you?	She kept everything the same apart from the size of the parachute canopy.
3	Remember the key facts.	A parachute with a large area will have greater air friction than a small parachute.
4	Work through the problem.	Was the height always the same? Tell how has the parachute size affected the fall?

SCIENTIFIC ENQUIRY

Making predictions

Achieved? 😊 😐 ☹

At Level 4, before you start an experiment, you will be asked to think about what will happen and predict the results.

Let's practise!

Cameron is testing the strength of different strips of paper. His teacher asks him to predict which one will be the strongest.

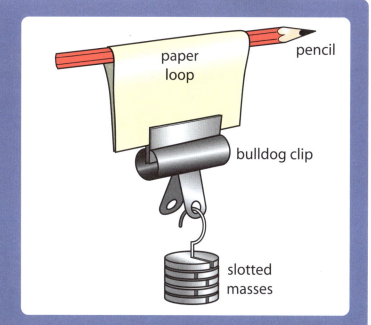

a) Which factors should he think about? Tick two.

☐ The colour of the paper.
☐ The thickness of the paper.
☐ The width of the paper.
☐ The length of the paper.

b) What should Cameron measure?

☐ How long before the strip tears, in seconds.
☐ How much mass tears the strip, in kilograms (kg).
☐ How long the paper strip is, in centimetres (cm).

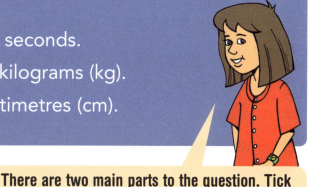

① Read the question then read it again. — There are two main parts to the question. Tick two boxes in the first part of the question and tick one box in the second part.

② Think about the question. What does it tell you? — Cameron is testing to see what mass the paper will carry.

③ Remember the key facts. — The variable that affects this is the strength of the paper. The colour is not important, but for a fair test, the strips should be the same width.

④ Work through the problem. — Are the other variables the same? Is the same width and length of the paper used?

SCIENTIFIC ENQUIRY

Patterns in data

At Level 4 you will be asked to spot patterns in data, for example, you will need to interpret bar charts.

Let's practise!

This chart shows the number of plants found in grassy places.

a) Where are most plants found?

b) Where are the fewest plants found? There are two places.

c) Why are fewer plants found in these two places?

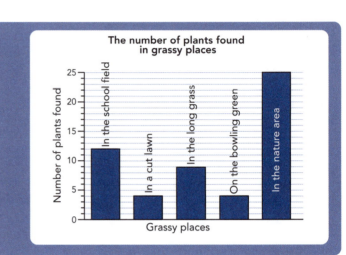

① Read the question then read it again. — You are only being asked to find three pieces of information from the chart.

② Think about the question. What does it tell you? — The place is along the bottom and the number of plants up the side.

③ Remember the key facts. — The taller the column, the greater the number of plants.

④ Work through the problem. — Look at all parts of the question. There are fewer plants where the grass is cut regularly.

There are two main sorts of graphs and charts.

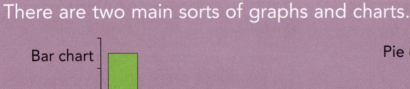
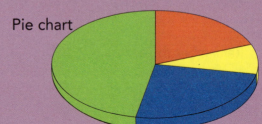

Bar chart — The taller the column, the greater the amount.

Pie chart — The bigger the piece of pie, the greater the amount.

SCIENTIFIC ENQUIRY

Explaining patterns in data

Achieved?

At Level 4 you will be asked to explain patterns in data, for example, saying that one factor depends on another.

Let's practise!

Look at this chart. It shows how far a toy car rolled down a ramp onto a carpet.

The height of the ramp above the carpet was changed. Explain the pattern you see in the chart.

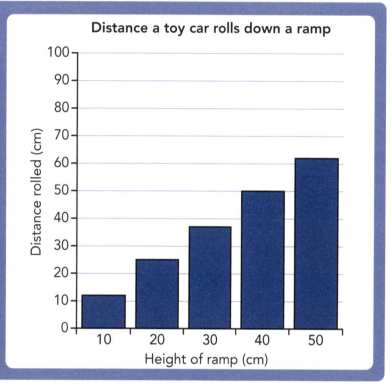

1 Read the question then read it again. — **You are being asked to explain the chart.**

2 Think about the question. What does it tell you? — **Five heights of ramp were tried and the distance a toy car rolled was measured.**

3 Remember the key facts. — **The higher the toy car is up the ramp, the greater the stored energy.**

4 Work through the problem. — **The toy rolled further as the height of the ramp was increased. The distance travelled depended on the height of the ramp. For example, the higher the ramp, the further it rolled.**

| Tip | ★ Look carefully at graphs to see whether you can see a pattern. Check to see whether there are any exceptions to the pattern. |

SCIENTIFIC ENQUIRY

Making sense of graphs

Achieved?

At Level 4 you will have to spot patterns in graphs.

Let's practise!

Ravi tested how long it took sugar to dissolve in water at different temperatures.

Here is the graph he made.

Use the graph to help.

a) How long did it take for the sugar to dissolve in water at 30°C?

b) How long did it take the sugar to dissolve in water at 40°C?

c) Explain the pattern you can see in this graph.

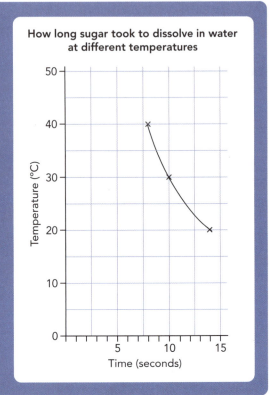

1 Read the question then read it again.

In the first two questions simply look at the graph. The third part asks you to work out the pattern.

2 Think about the question.

A line graph tells a story.

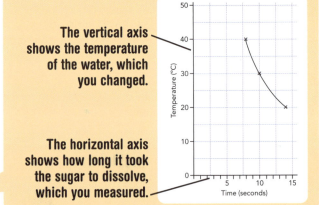

The vertical axis shows the temperature of the water, which you changed.

The horizontal axis shows how long it took the sugar to dissolve, which you measured.

3 Remember the key facts.

Sugar dissolves more quickly in warm water than it does in cooler water.

4 Work through the problem.

What are the times and temperatures involved? Where can you read this from the graph?

SCIENTIFIC ENQUIRY

Plotting line graphs

Achieved?

At Level 4 you will be asked to plot line graphs.

Let's practise!

Sophie was testing spinners to see how quickly they fell. She attached different masses and timed how quickly each fell.

Mass on spinner	5 g	10 g	15 g
Time taken to fall 2 m	4 seconds	3 seconds	2 seconds

Mark the three results on the graph paper.
Join up the marks to make a line graph.

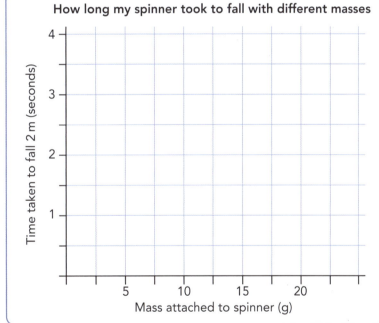

How long my spinner took to fall with different masses

1	Read the question then read it again.	**You have to plot three points on the graph paper.**
2	Think about the question. What does it tell you?	**There is a connection between the weight of a spinner and the time it takes to fall.**
3	Remember the key facts.	**Heavier spinners fall faster than light spinners.**
4	Work through the problem.	**Start by looking at the bottom axis and find 5 g. Go up until you reach 4 seconds. Make a cross. Do the same for 10 g and 15 g. Join the crosses to make a line graph.**

BREADTH OF STUDY

Medicines and drugs

Achieved?

At Level 4 you will know that medicines can be harmful if you take them incorrectly.

Let's practise!

Decide which of the statements about medicines and drugs are true or false. Place a tick in the box if true, and a cross if false.

- ☐ Medicines can have bad effects on humans.
- ☐ If you maintain a healthy lifestyle you will never need to take medicine.
- ☐ Medicines are not drugs.
- ☐ You should never put a medicine inside a jar that a toddler could open.
- ☐ All drugs are harmful.
- ☐ You should only take medicines in the quantities and at times prescribed by the doctor.

① Read the question then read it again. — These questions are all about the effects of drugs, their storage and their safe use.

② Remember the key facts. — All medicines are drugs, but not all drugs are medicines.

③ Work through the problem. — Apply your knowledge of drugs and medicines to the questions.

Remember that some drugs can be harmful but others can improve your health, combat disease and even keep people alive.

BREADTH OF STUDY

Micro-organisms

 Achieved?

At level 4 you will know that micro-organisms are living organisms that are often too small to be seen.

Let's practise!

Ian claims that micro-organisms can break down all materials easily. Jackie disagrees and says that some materials take thousands of years to break down.

Look at the objects in the table below. Which ones can be broken down quickly by micro-organisms and which ones take more than 50 years?

 glass bottle
 potato peelings

Can be broken down by micro-organisms

 grass cuttings
 aluminium drinks can

 leaves on the ground
 dead mouse

Cannot be broken down by micro-organisms within 50 years

 disposable nappy
 plastic container

① Read the question then read it again.

Look at the list of objects.

② Think about the question. What does it tell you?

Start with the ones you know for sure. Dead leaves, grass cuttings and potato peelings all get put into compost bins.

③ Remember the key facts.

Micro-organisms can break things down. Some of our waste products are made of materials that biodegrade easily while others will last for thousands of years. Other materials take longer to biodegrade, like plastic, metals and glass. Join up the objects with the correct box.

④ Work through the problem.

When you have decided about each item, join it to the correct statement.

Micro-organisms can be both beneficial and harmful. They are useful when they break down materials.

How long does it take for materials to decompose? Plastic bags take more than 100 years. Aluminium takes up to 500 years and glass doesn't decompose so it will probably still be here in millions of years.

BREADTH OF STUDY

Important scientists

Achieved?

At Level 4 you will be able to recognise some important scientists and understand why they are famous.

Let's practise!

Read this information about Florence Nightingale.

You might not think that Florence Nightingale was a scientist. You might think of her as a nurse. But although she died a hundred years ago, she changed nursing and hospitals for ever. In 1854, she and 38 nurses set out for a huge hospital in Turkey. There were hundreds of wounded soldiers from the Crimean War crowded into the hospital: British, French, Russian and Turkish. More than half died of their wounds. Florence's team cleaned and scrubbed the hospital, gave out food and medicine, and cleaned and bandaged soldiers' wounds. Six months later, hardly any soldiers were dying. Later, Florence changed the design of other hospitals to big, clean, airy 'Nightingale Wards'.

> Why did cleaning the hospital and the soldiers' wounds stop many of them dying?

1 Read the information carefully.

The Nightingale nurses 'cleaned and scrubbed the hospital, gave out food and medicine, and cleaned and bandaged soldiers' wounds'.

2 Look for the information you need.

The cleaning will have killed harmful micro-organisms or 'germs' that infected and killed the injured soldiers. Medicines and food were also important for getting better, but you are not asked about them.

3 Work through the problem.

It's important to answer that some micro-organisms are harmful; these 'germs' cause infection which could spread easily in a crowded hospital.

Some micro-organisms are helpful. They are essential to decay – and even to making some kinds of food.

Some micro-organisms are harmful. They cause diseases, and can spread diseases (infection) between people.

Cleaning kills many micro-organisms and reduces the spread of infection.

Tip ★ When you are given a lot of information, look carefully for the facts that answer the question. You can learn from the rest as well, of course!

KEY TOPICS

Scientific Enquiry (Sc1)

At Level 3 you need to be able to:

- put forward your own ideas to answer a question
- know why it is important to gather data to answer questions
- make observations
- use simple measuring equipment
- carry out a fair test with help
- record observations in a variety of ways
- explain observations
- suggest improvements to your work

At Level 4 you need to be able to:

- see that you need evidence to support scientific ideas
- decide on the best way to do an experiment or test
- make good predictions
- select the most important information
- choose the best equipment for a test
- record observations and measurements
- draw and make sense of a bar chart
- come to conclusions
- say ways in which work can be improved

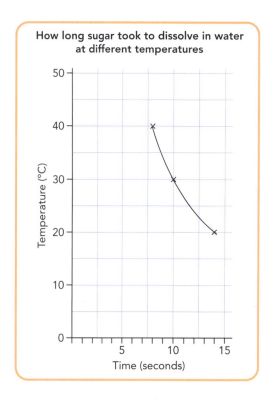

At Level 5 you need to be able to:

- explain scientific ideas
- choose the best information
- choose the right equipment to make measurements
- use the equipment correctly
- repeat measurements
- explain why there might be differences between measurements of the same thing
- understand line graphs
- draw line graphs
- suggest ways in which work could be improved
- use scientific ways to communicate ideas

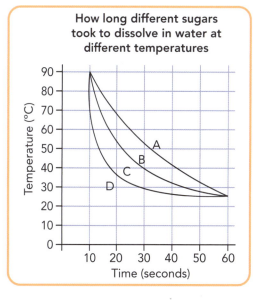

KEY TOPICS

Life processes and living things (Sc2)

At Level 3 you need to know:

- about basic life processes
- the differences between living and non-living things
- reasons for changes in living things, such as diet and water supply
- the ways in which animals are suited to their environment

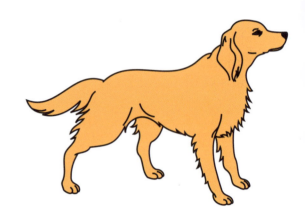

At Level 4 you need to know:

- the names of some of the organs of the human body
- the position of some of the organs of the human body
- the names and position of some of the organs of a variety of plants
- how to use simple keys to identify living things
- how to put living things into groups
- about food chains

At Level 5 you need to know:

- the jobs done by some of the organs in the human body
- the jobs done by some of the organs in plants
- about the life cycles of humans and some other animals
- about the life cycles of plants
- how to classify some living things
- that living things are found in places that suit them

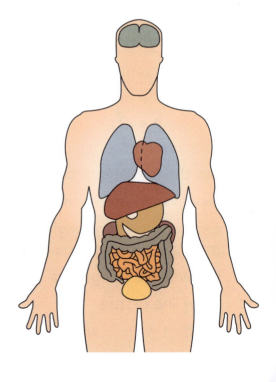

KEY TOPICS

Materials and their properties (Sc3)

At Level 3 you need to know:

- how to put forward your own ideas to answer a question
- about sorting materials into groups
- why some materials are suited to a particular purpose
- which changes can be reversed
- which changes cannot be reversed

At Level 4 you need to know:

- that you need evidence to support scientific ideas
- about the properties of materials
- how materials are classified into solids, liquids and gases
- how to separate simple mixtures
- the scientific words used to describe changes, such as condense, evaporate and freeze
- which changes are easily reversed and which changes are difficult to reverse

At Level 5 you need to know:

- the properties of metals
- the ways in which metals differ from other solids
- the ways in which changes, such as evaporation and condensation, take place
- how to separate mixtures of materials

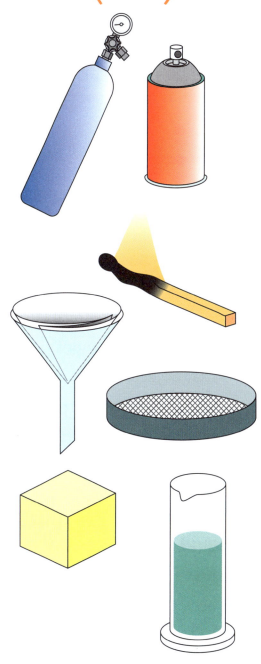

Physical processes (Sc4)

At Level 3 you need to know:

- the causes and effects in physical processes, such as a bulb not lighting because of a break in the circuit
- about forces changing the direction or speed of movement
- the effects of sound and light, such as the way they get fainter as the sources become more distant

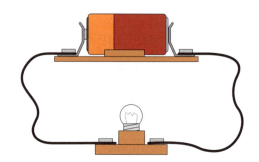

At Level 4 you need to know:

- how to alter electrical circuits
- how the Sun changes position during the day
- that objects are attracted by gravity
- which things are attracted by magnets
- that magnets can attract and repel each other
- how shadows are formed
- that sounds travel through a variety of materials

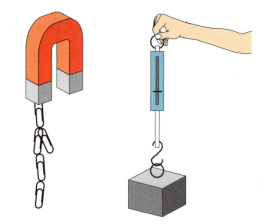

At Level 5 you need to know:

- how to alter the current flowing in a circuit
- about the effect of adding bulbs to a series circuit
- about the effect of adding and subtracting cells from a circuit
- how to measure forces
- that forces operate in particular directions
- how to draw circuits using symbols
- how to change the pitch and loudness of a sound
- that vibrations result in sounds
- that the light from objects passes into your eyes
- about the orbit of the Earth and the Moon
- how to use knowledge of orbits to explain the length of the day and year

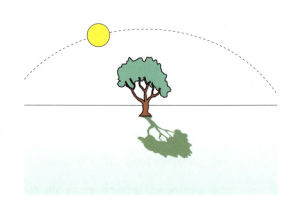

Answers

Page 11 – Explaining results
a) Day 4

b) Day 16

c) There will probably never be 20 seedlings as it is unlikely that all seeds will sprout.

Page 12 – Living and non-living things
The following should be joined to the child:
It can move by itself.
It breathes.
It will grow into an adult.

The following should be joined to the doll:
It does not eat.
It will not grow at all.

Page 13 – Variables affecting plant growth
a) The seedlings in Tray B.

b) The seedlings in Tray A.

c) The same amount of water was given to each tray.

d) The cupboard would have been darker and therefore the seedlings would have grown faster as they searched for light. They would have been less healthy and spindly, yellow and pale.

Page 14 – Grouping materials
a) Brass and steel conduct electricity.
Wood and plastic do not conduct electricity.

b) Steel and iron are magnetic.
Glass and aluminium are non-magnetic.

Page 15 – Uses of materials
glass, transparent, windows
copper, electrical conductor, electrical wires
rubber, high friction and hard wearing, bike tyres
cotton, soft and warm to the touch, clothes
stone, heavy and hard, garden walls

Page 16 – Reversible and non-reversible changes
Change which is reversible: freezing water and heating ice.

Change which is not reversible: burning wood, firing pottery in a kiln, frying an egg and baking a cake.

Page 17 – How we see things
a) Box 3 should be ticked because the diagram shows light reflected in all directions.

b) Only some of the light enters the eye of the person looking at the bulb.

Page 18 – Pushes and pulls
a)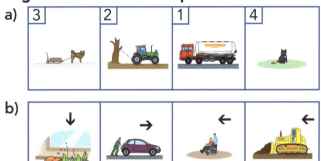

b)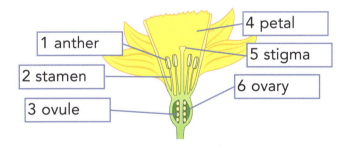

Page 19 – Flower parts
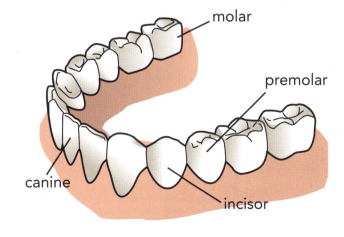

Page 20 – Teeth and eating

ANSWERS

Incisors – for cutting food
Canines – for holding and tearing food
Premolars – for grinding and crushing food
Molars – for grinding and crushing food

Page 21 – Human organs

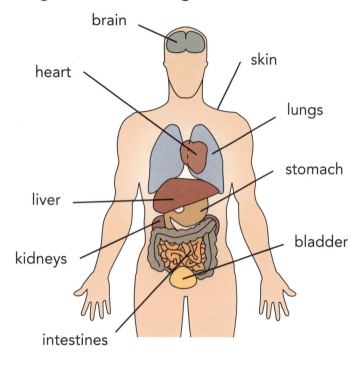

Page 22 – Living processes

a) Bonfire is the odd one out as it is not living.

b) We know plants are alive because they grow, produce seeds, and use sunlight, water and air to make food.

Page 23 – Classification

Mammal dog, lion
Bird eagle, vulture
Reptile tortoise, crocodile
Insect bee, butterfly

Page 24 – Keys

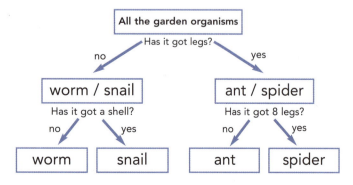

Page 25 – Animals in their environment

shark: oceans, streamlined body
penguin: icy land and cold seas, waterproof feathers
camel: desert, long eyelashes
giraffe: grasslands, long neck so they can feed from the tree tops

Page 26 – Predators and prey

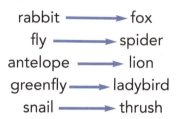

Page 27 – Food chains

a) Sun ➔ grass ➔ rabbit ➔ fox

b) Snail/slug or other common animal

Page 28 – Thermal insulators and conductors

Of the three materials, metal is the best thermal conductor so heat can travel through it most easily. The pottery cup is a fairly good thermal conductor and some heat passes through. The polystyrene is a very poor conductor of heat and therefore it lets the least amount of heat pass through it.

Page 29 – Gases

Gases take the shape of their container.
Gases fill the space available.

Page 30 – Making mixtures

a) Tick 'salt' and 'brown sugar'.

b) Tick 'stir the mixture' and 'use hot water'.

Page 31 – Separating mixtures

When stirred, the salt and water dissolved.

Overnight the water had evaporated, leaving the salt in the saucer.

Page 32 – Sieving and filtering

a) Kelly's mum should use a sieve to separate the stones from the soil.

b) The filter paper lets the juice through, but traps the bits in the orange juice.

ANSWERS

Page 33 – Solid, liquid and gas

a)

Solid at room temperature	Liquid at room temperature	Gas at room temperature
stone ice cream paper chocolate	oil milk shampoo	oxygen helium hydrogen

b) Two solid foods could include cereals, sugar, bread and fruit.

Two liquid foods could include milk, fruit juice and water.

Page 34 – Evaporation

a) The water on the windowsill will evaporate most quickly. The water in the fridge will evaporate most slowly.

b) Water will evaporate more quickly from a container in a warm place.

Page 35 – Air resistance

a) The scrunched up paper will hit the ground first because it will be affected less by air resistance. The flat sheet of paper will be affected more by air resistance and will therefore fall more slowly.

b) The larger ball will be more affected by air resistance and will travel a shorter distance than the tighter, smaller ball.

Page 36 – Magnetic attraction and repulsion

The red and blue ends will attract.

The two blue ends will repel.

The two red ends will repel.

Page 37 – Magnetic sorting

Metals attracted to magnets	Metals not attracted to magnets
iron steel	copper silver aluminium

Page 38 – Making electrical circuits

1) normal   2) dim
3) bright   4) off

Page 39 – Electrical switches

a) 1) ✓
   2) ✗
   3) ✓
   4) ✓

b) Own answer

Page 40 – The position of the Sun

a)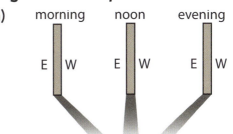

b) The Earth turns on its axis.

Page 41 – Gravity

a) Tub of clay

b) Newtons

c) Gravity

Page 42 – Friction

a) Sara is correct.

b) Friction is acting upon the car and preventing it from moving. The force of friction is created between the tyres of the car and the ramp.

Page 43 – Friction forces

a) Gravity pulled the slide down the runway.

b) The toy may slide more slowly, or not at all, because there will be more friction.

Page 44 – The size of shadows

The clown's shadow will be shorter because the light source is higher.

Page 45 – Opaque, transparent and translucent

a) The book makes a dark shadow because it is opaque and the light is being blocked.

The bottle makes a faint shadow because it is transparent and light will pass through it.

b) glass window   T   mirror   O
   brick wall   O   jam jar   T
   bathroom window   TL   tissue paper   TL

ANSWERS

Page 46 – Sounds we hear

Jim can hold it firmly to stop the triangle vibrating.

The vibration of the drum skin causes the beads to jump up and down.

Sound get fainter the further you are away from the source.

Page 47 – Sounds through different materials

a) The sound is travelling through the air.

b) Leo can hear the sounds better through the table than he can through the air.

c) The scarf absorbs sound so Leo is not able to hear the sound.

Page 48 – Questions in an experiment

a) Do parachutes with a larger surface area fall more slowly than those with a smaller surface area?

b) The larger the surface area of the parachute the greater the time taken for the parachute to fall 1 metre.

Page 49 – Making predictions

a) The thickness of the paper.
   The width of the paper.

b) How much mass tears the strip, in kilograms (kg).

Page 50 – Patterns in data

a) Most plants were found in the nature area.

b) The fewest plants were found in the cut lawn and on the bowling green.

c) There were fewer plants found here because the grass is cut more regularly in these two places.

Page 51 – Explaining patterns in data

The toy rolled further as the height of the ramp increased.

Page 52 – Making sense of graphs

a) 10 seconds

b) 8 seconds

c) The pattern that you see in the graph is that sugar dissolves more quickly in warm water than it does in cold water.

Page 53 – Plotting line graphs

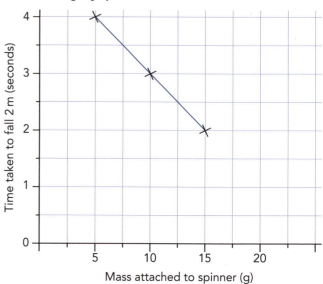

Page 54 – Medicines and drugs

True
False
False
True
False
True

Page 55 – Micro-organisms

Can be broken down by micro-organisms
Dead mouse
Leaves on the ground
Potato peelings
Grass cuttings

Cannot be broken down by micro-organisms
Glass bottle
Disposable nappy
Aluminium drinks can
Plastic container

Page 56 – Important scientists – Florence Nightingale

Harmful micro-organisms or 'germs' caused infection and could easily spread in crowded hospitals. The cleaning killed the harmful micro-organisms and reduced infection amongst injured soldiers.